This Journal Belongs To

19618677R00063

Made in the USA
Lexington, KY
29 November 2018